YOUNG WOMAN'S GUIDE

YETUNDE A. ODUGBESAN-OMEDE

ISBN-10: 0692322957

ISBN-13: 978-0692322956

For more information contact Yetunde Odugbesan-Omede at

yetunde.ao@gmail.com

Visit the website: www.yetundeodugbesan.com
www.youngwomansguide.org

ACKNOWLEDGMENTS

I would like to thank my parents, Chief Mr. & Mrs Adewale and Biola Odugbesan for their unconditional love, constant encouragement and raising me to dream big and follow my passions. To my mother, Biola Odugbesan, for teaching me how to be a leader and a woman of substance; to my husband Osahon, my best friend and confidant for his undying love and support; to my son, Amadin, my angel who blessed me with the role of a lifetime of being his mother; to my big brother, Abi, whom I admire dearly and look up to; to my mentors and dear friends who believed in me and always supported my dreams—thank you!

Thank you all for equipping me with the tools I need to make a difference in this world and in the lives of others.

Table of Contents

INTRODUCTION

Dear Greatness,

The journey of womanhood is truly a unique experience; however, I have gained some valuable jewels and wisdom during the course of my ongoing journey that I would like to share with you.

I strongly believe that, as a young woman, in order to be a successful leader or to accomplish the goals you have set for yourself, you must have what I call the 3 P's—passion, purpose and perseverance. This book was written out of my passion and purpose to empower people to excel and live a meaningful life. I am excited to share my own personal stories and advice on how to put your best self forward.

This book is dedicated to you and every young woman around the world who is striving to make a difference, become a woman of substance and most importantly, discover her own purpose. It is my hope that after reading this book you are better equipped and empowered as you continue on the journey of womanhood.

Purposefully,

Yetunde

1

PASSION AND PURPOSE

Passion leads to purpose.
The moment you are able to realize
your true passion you are one step
closer to achieving your
life's purpose.

P assion leads to purpose. The moment you are able to realize your true Passion you are one step closer to achieving your life's purpose. What is passion? Passion is an intense desire or emotion for something. Passion provides us with focus, clarity and direction. Most importantly passion pushes us to fulfill our fullest potential. Knowing what your passionate about is becoming increasingly important for one's personal and professional success.

For me, my passion is what empowers me, and my purpose is why I wrote this book. My passion is to motivate, to empower and to encourage. This passion encourages, empowers and motivates me to fulfill my purpose.

What is purpose? Purpose is the reason for which something exists. Now I ask you a very big question, "Why do you exist?" Here's a simple answer to a complex question: to make a difference. Each and every one of us is created for a purpose; to do something only you can fulfill. Philosopher Osho says, "Each person comes into this world with a specific destiny—he or she has something to fulfill, some message has to be delivered, some work has to be completed. You are not here accidentally—you are here meaningfully. There is a purpose behind you. The whole world intends to do something through you." What a powerful statement!

What you are doing right now at this very moment is preparing you for your destined roles of tomorrow. Finding your purpose is not about giving back in a grandiose way. It is about turning your skills, talents and gifts into the form of service. We often commit our time and talent to causes or activities that speak to our interest and specifically our life's mission.

I have learned that in order to truly be successful, you must first find what you are passionate about. Passion will always serve as your compass to finding your purpose. We often confuse success with the fulfillment of purpose. Remember being successful does not mean you have fulfilled your life's purpose. You can be successful at something that has absolutely nothing to do with your sole purpose, calling, or mission. True success is the fulfillment of your purpose. The only way to find true success is when you find what you are truly and uniquely passionate about.

We all struggle with trying to figure out our purpose and what our impact on this world will be. But we forget that everyone on this earth will be given their own epiphany, their own time to shine and most importantly an opportunity to live out their destiny. There is an appointed time of discovery and impact for everyone. Everyone has his or her own time and space in history.

You cannot escape your purpose; however, the decisions that you make can sometimes alter or throw you off track. It's important to make decisions that will move you closer to living a life of meaning and service. There are so many people counting on you to fulfill your purpose. The success and freedom of others is predicated on your existence and following through with your purpose. The world needs you.

INVEST IN
YOURSELF

While we work on ourselves so that we can continue to become a better person, we in turn add to the welfare of society while reaching the apex of personal development.

I believe that you are your own project and the type of life you live will be your grade. There is one main project in life that we should pursue which is the project of constant investment in our professional and personal development. The project of working on oneself to the point of excellence is a choice that I am a faithful advocate of. The project of constant self-improvement and searching for who you are as a person can never be a futile pursuit.

While we work on ourselves so that we can continue to become a better person, we in turn, add to the welfare of society while reaching the apex of personal development. Look at investing into yourself as a form of preparing for the next big thing that may come your way. You never know when the next opportunity may come that may change your life, so it is best to be prepared. Your education, internships, jobs, volunteer experience, leadership development and more are all forms of investment.

Life comes in stages, and each stage is a preparation for the next. Everyone wants success, but are you prepared for it? Are you currently in a position to receive it? Opportunity presents itself in many disguises, but we often turn it away due to feelings of uncertainty or not being "prepared" enough to take such opportunity.

Preparedness comes in various forms. If you have a desire to start a business, then do your research beforehand. Are your finances somewhat in order? Have you sought out advice on what steps you need to take? Have you invested the time and effort needed to turn your goals into fruition? Investing in yourself also means that you are taking a conscious effort to surround yourself with people who are interested in your personal and professional development.

Life essentially involves preparation—preparing for a job, preparing for marriage, preparing for children and so forth. We are in a constant state of habitual preparation, yet there are so many instances when opportunity knocks and we don't open the door. Why? There are some opportunities that will come once in a lifetime and some, if you are lucky enough, will appear again. Will you be ready when opportunity knocks? Will you be able to discern and decipher what the opportunity is? Or will you miss out? Life is all about seizing opportunities, making the right decisions and being prepared. Education prepares you, training prepares you, and research prepares you—so that you will be ready when the opportunity of your lifetime finds you. I can't emphasize enough how important it is to map out your short and long-term goals and strategies on how you plan to get there and how you plan to use every opportunity to its full advantage. Author Orison Swett Marden said, "Opportunities? They are all around us, there is power lying latent everywhere waiting for the observant eye to discover it." You may not know it but there are opportunities, gifts, business proposals, divine meetings, great experiences and more that are coming to you, so invest and prepare yourself! Be ready and be open to expect great things. The world needs you at your best, so you must put every effort into putting your best self forward. Each stage in life is an opportunity to prepare for the next. Prepare yourself for greatness! Read the bios of your favorite leaders or people who inspire you, and you will realize how much they have invested and put the work into reaching such heights

Opportunities do not come very often, but when they do you must learn how to recognize and take advantage of them. People will come into your life in the strangest ways and obscure reasons, but their presence has a definite purpose. Too many times we meet people during networking events, conferences, at work, at school and social events and do not recognize the opportunities they present. Try not to be closed minded when it comes to picking and choosing opportunities. It is a blessing to have options. Be open to trying different things, internships, careers and more. But always have an end goal or a vision of where you want to be. Some of us dream of being a doctor, lawyer, writer, investment banker, social worker and much more and we stick to that path. We tend to forget about our other passions or goals. We at times believe that focusing on too many goals may leave one confused, overwhelmed or distracted from one's primary goal. So, some of us begin to believe that it is safer to just do one thing and do it well. Life is all about living abundantly and exploring options for you.

It is possible be an investment banker, writer, painter, social activist and much more. When we live out our different passions, we are fully experiencing the totality of who we are. We become smarter, wiser and fulfilled because we are nurturing the very areas in our lives that we tend to neglect. By creating and exploring options for ourselves in regards to our academic, professional and personal areas, we in turn create *opportunities* of possible successes and profits. You never know, you may be in medical school but have a great talent for interior design. That untapped talent could become a profitable and successful skill once nurtured. So, create options for yourself. Do not believe the idea that one goal takes you farther away from accomplishing the other. Look at them as separate goals, and go after them. As we continue to nurture the various gifts and talents that we possess we are essentially preparing ourselves to seize more opportunities.

THERE IS NO COMPARISON

Accepting yourself for who you are is the greatest gift you can give yourself.

Why compare yourself to others? There is no comparison. We compare our lives to others constantly, whether unknowingly or knowingly. We measure ourselves against other women's timelines, other women's successes and life choices. Everyone has their own divine timeline, their own journey to success, their own purpose, their own destiny, their own way of living, their own way of expressing themselves, their own way of communication—everyone is different.

Accepting yourself for who you are is the greatest gift you can give yourself. Accepting yourself means that you are fully aware of your gifts, flaws, talents, skills, behavior and attitude. Accepting who are you gives you the courage and strength to maintain your own sense of self. A large part of not comparing yourself to others is being secure with the person you are.

By focusing on others, you miss out on making your own mark and impact. By focusing on other people's timeline, you miss out on your own divine opportunities and experiences. By focusing on someone else's purpose and way of ministry, you may miss your own calling. Why waste time focusing on someone else when the world should be focusing on you? Every second you have here on earth should be spent in cultivating your mission, achieving your goals, finding your purpose so that if someone wanted to compare themselves to you, it should bring them closer to their authentic self, not further away from it. It should inspire them to dream more and do more. Be an excellent version of yourself rather than a second best version of someone else.

In order to be an excellent version of yourself you have to purposefully set out to achieve a goal that is unique to you. At times as young women, it's easy to look at someone else's style or profession and end up re-creating the wheel. But the true testament of life is finding what you are good at. It's finding your voice and purpose. Work on creating something more innovative, creative and distinctive to you. Follow your own dreams not those of someone else. Don't do it because the person next to you has done it; do it because it speaks to who you are. Excellence is born out of originality, consistency and passion. As a young woman, you are needed by the world to be excellent. Your excellence is what will one day change the life of someone else.

Life needs more women who are willing to lead the pack rather than follow it. It needs more women who are genuine in their approaches and truly seek to make society a better place. We all need your individuality and uniqueness. Remember no one can compete against individuality—

everyone has it but hardly uses it. Your trademark, imprint and legacy are to be who you are. Be who you are and do it well, extremely well. Be an excellent version of yourself. Say to yourself: today I will start to do everything I once planned to do. Today I will begin to change everything I once planned to change. And today, I will start by changing myself. I will put into action every desire, every opportunity and every goal that I have set before myself.

As a young woman, always remember that you are the one and only, wonderfully made, equal to the task, perfect with each step, stronger with each walk, authentic from head to toe. There is no comparison to you. Like everyone else, you have much to offer. The, world awaits you! Show the world who you are, why you are here and what you have to offer. Don't down rate, downgrade or downsize yourself because of anyone. Don't compare yourself to others; rather be inspired or empowered by them, and use them as an example to better something that you like about yourself. Every day look into the mirror and say something to yourself that you like about yourself, out loud. Or if you like to write, write little positive sticky notes about yourself and leave them where you can see them. Focus on the things that make you unique and beautiful. This will build your self-esteem and confidence in your own abilities and direction. Be content with yourself and your abilities. Sometimes people tend to compare their skills or abilities with those of others. They compare their personal lives, their professions, their academic attainments and lifestyles with those of other people. Such comparison may foster unhealthy competition, breed insecurity and cause one to be covetous. We must learn to be content in the accomplishments of our goals. We must believe that our best is good enough. It is important for young women to understand that their lifestyles and decisions should be made according to what is best for them as an individual. Strive for excellence, but do so because there is a higher reason and a purpose behind it. Be content in your personal, spiritual, academic and professional areas of your life. The position where you may be in life is not permanent. Be patient everything that is meant for you will come into fruition. Remember contentment does not mean complacence.

Contentment means to be at peace. It means that you trust your own abilities and power to accomplish anything you put your mind and heart to. It also means that you understand the process of life and not everything happens all at once. Success is a journey that has resting points.

Here are six steps that I believe will bring you closer to contentment and loving your own unique identity:

1. Realize how lucky you are.
Not everyone is as fortunate as you.

2. Be thankful for what you have.
Sit back and think about everything you have, not from a material standpoint. When you look at things from such a standpoint, one will always see what they do not have and will always seek to want more. But when you realize that you already have the most essential and necessary things like food, water, shelter, and clothes and loved ones, there is no reason not to be happy.

3. You are not other people.
You are your own person with your own dreams and goals. You have to make sure that you understand that things will happen for you accordingly; it may not be today but some day.

4. Do not confuse being content with being complacent.
You can still be content and still continue to work hard in the pursuit of your goals.

5. Every one's time is different.
Successes come at different times.
Do not clock yourself. Many times, people have a tendency to put a time limit on the completion of their goals. And when these things do not happen according to the time they have set for themselves, it is easy to become disappointed.
There is a divine time and place for everything.

6. All is well. Remember everything is working for your good, so be at peace.
Be content and okay with your current position. Still work hard in the fruition of your goals, but understand that everything will be okay. So when you look at other people's lives, those blessings or seasons was created just for them and there is one created just for you.

JEALOUSY

Jealousy, whether received or projected, is harmful.

"You become more and more artificial. Imitating others, competing with others, what else can you do? If somebody has something and you don't have it, and you don't have a natural possibility of having it, the only way is to have some cheap substitute for it."-Osho

Now what is the root cause of jealousy and how does one overcome it? Root causes to jealousy are growing insecurities, lack of self-esteem and confidence, competitiveness (a belief that you must compete with others to be successful), a reduced level of self-love, always comparing yourself, your accomplishments, your material possessions, your family structure, your relationships and more to those of others. Being in a state of jealousy, the pre-development of full-blown envy, is caused by possessiveness, a lack of knowledge or awareness about who you are, and last not but least, not being alert to your inner emotions or thoughts. These root causes must be identified and dealt with one by one. The person who fills his or her receptacle with envious thoughts will end up living a non-satisfied life, in constant torment and unhappiness, because for jealous people, nothing is ever enough.

A jealous person is an illustration of deeply rooted issues that have consumed his or her way of thinking and acting. A jealous person does not realize that their destiny, purpose, timing, mission, and over-all life experiences are solely unique and incomparable. They believe that the goodness in your life takes away or continues to diminish the goodness or possibilities in their life. So the higher you rise, the bigger you get and the more relevant you are, in their minds you are somehow or in some way an obstacle to their possibilities for success.

Jealous people do not know that there is enough room in the garden for every flower; they would rather kill your growth and that of others to make room for themselves (signs of selfishness). The pre-development of jealousy is envy. At first envy is the feeling of wanting or coveting someone else's belongings. If these feelings are not dealt with over time, they turn into full-blown jealousy, which turns into hatred. You see, envious people want your outward signs of success; jealous people want your inner workings. They would rather give up their own personality, behavior, spirituality and attitude in order to become you. Beware of friends, family-members, associates, colleagues, and more who exhibit these traits. An experience of projected jealousy can harm you; you don't deserve to be mistreated or diminished by someone else's lack of self-appreciation.

In order to overcome jealousy one must understand that every life is incomparable and unique. Envy is an emotion that everyone experiences, but one must have the power to control it. You have to be alert when it comes to your emotions. You cannot let your emotions overpower you and turn you into someone that you were never meant to be. Self-love may be the cure to all emotional sickness. Every now and then sit back and think about how great you are, how unique and distinctive you are, what talents and skills you have and how your life makes a difference. At a young age we are all taught to be competitive. You must be alert though, and tuned in to your emotions when you see competitiveness turning into envy. There are two types of competitive people. Person # 1 competes to be better than someone else, so for him or her, achievement or success is based on someone else's level of achievement. Person # 2 competes to better himself. He or she races side-by-side with others and competes with themselves pushing their own limits, self-learning as they go. Having a real knowledge about who you are is the key to everything. When you know yourself and who you want to be, you will never let your emotions overcome you . . .. Because when you love yourself enough, there will be no room for envy or jealousy.

BEWARE OF DREAM KILLERS

Be careful whom you tell your dreams to because a negative response can be damaging to the birth of that dream.

It's a harsh but very real reality that not everyone is going to like you. In fact, there will be people out there whose mission is to destroy and break down everything you work so hard to achieve. Even more frightening, there are people out there who can sense and smell potential Or what I like to call Purpose. Beware and stay clear of these people.

You cannot get through life without opposition. When you have a purpose you will face all types of obstacles, but do not let it get to you. Here's why:

- Your purpose on this earth is far greater than any opposition you will face.
- Where there is light there is also darkness.
- Your potential or purpose will intimidate others.
- Don't take it personally. It comes with the territory when striving for excellence.

When you have a dream that is deep within you there is also a powerful potential that comes with realizing that dream. It is only when you act upon turning that dream into reality that you will begin to witness some push back. Opposition may arise in various forms. It could be through your friends who try to belittle your dreams or mentors who believe their course for your own life is the only route to success. It could be in the form of jealousy and envy from people closest to you. It can also come in the form of fear, doubt and anxiousness. I always tell women both young and seasoned to be careful whom you tell your dreams to because a negative response can be damaging to the birth of that dream. Not everyone is happy for you! It's the plain truth. No matter how nice or loving you are, not everyone will be happy for you, especially when you start to turn your dreams into reality and begin achieving your goals. There are so many people who have been discouraged from achieving their dreams, all because someone downplayed it or plotted and competed against it. Poet Langston Hughes once said, "A dream deferred is like a broken wing bird that cannot fly."

Do not, I repeat, give up on your dreams because of the opinions of others. Dreams are to be kept treasured and only shared with people who are like-minded and wish you well.

MENTORS

*We forget that mentors are humans
too, who are flawed and open
to human error.
Temper your expectations.*

A s you continue to grow both professionally and personally, you need to have someone you look up to, or aspire to be, become your mentor. Don't be afraid to seek out people whose professional achievements you admire. As a young woman, I am blessed to say that it was both men and women who devoted their time to mentor me. I would say that my mother was and still is my mentor. She is my lifelong mentor; however there are women who I can point to and say that they have played a major role in the achievements of my goals.

Before seeking out a mentor, ask yourself these three questions:
1. Am I drawn to this person because of his or her professional achievements only?
2. Are there certain qualities that my mentor has that I want to adopt?
3. Am I forming a relationship with this person to guide me professionally? Personally? Or both?

The reason why I say it's important to ask yourself these questions is because we often seek out mentors based on their outward persona or public accomplishments. Which means we seek out people who have something that we want or want to develop. She may be the CEO of a Fortune 500 company, she may be a medical doctor or lawyer or well-known author or artist. We use those outward signs and draw general conclusions that such person may also be able to build me up both professionally and personally because of the level of their success.

We forget that mentors are humans too, who are flawed and open to human error. For example, I had a mentor who I thought was just absolutely remarkable because I was fixated on the position and status; however, my expectations where sadly crushed when I realized as our relationship blossomed that we did not share the same values about family, success and many other things. I learned that mentorship comes in many forms, and I had to choose carefully in whom I confided and whom I chose to pour into my life. As a young woman its easy to latch unto every word and action your mentor advises you to do because your goal is to be like them, learn from them or perhaps be better than them. But if you don't have a secure sense of self-direction you may mistakenly adopt habits, values, thought processes that are not unique to you and that may actually inhibit your growth.

My advice to you is this: seek out mentors and learn from them; however, temper your expectations because he or she many not be able to give you what you need. And most importantly mentee and mentorship relationships have beginning and end points; know that certain relationships are only for a season.

It is important to be thankful for every person who comes into your life. Whether they come into your life to teach you or to show you who not become, they all serve a purpose and that purpose is to help you grow into a better person.

FINDING YOUR INNER STRENGTH

*When you look deep within yourself,
there lies a hidden compartment
where strength lives.*

Everything in life that happens to you, whether good or bad, is all for your benefit. When you look back on past events that almost stole your happiness, your trust and your whole being, you realize now that you did not die, but in fact you are alive and well. The aftermath of failure, depression, sickness, and disappointments are success, happiness, understanding, awareness and peace. Resolve in yourself and in your mind that nothing, absolutely nothing can stop you. That is when life begins.

You are unmovable and insurmountable. Nothing can take away your pride, happiness, success or your self-being without your permission. You must go through life with authority, believing that you can overcome anything and everything. Being an overcomer is a choice and a lifestyle. An overcomer is a person who goes through life with an understanding that everything happens for his or her own good.

I challenge you to be an overcomer today and to go through life with authority and to tap into your vault of strength. Show the world that you are indeed unstoppable. Remember that you have the power to change the direction of your life. Being an overcomer is a choice. It is a lifestyle.

Perseverance is what will separate you from the rest. The completion of your goals is not about how smart you are or how well connected you are—it's about your level of perseverance. Perseverance requires patience and passion. You must be patient with yourself and others regarding the completion of your goals. You must also have passion for what it is you want to achieve. A type of passion that is unbreakable regardless of what life may hurl at you. Success requires certain ingredients. It requires passion, purpose, faith, vision, focus, hard work, strategic decision-making and most of all perseverance. You may have all the requirements to be a success but if you cannot endure or persevere in order to see your plans into fruition, then you have missed the mark.

Perseverance is the answer to life's challenges. Life is unpredictable and presents many challenges, obstacles, and experiences, yet if you can persevere through it all, you will be able to see the glory of life. People give up on their dreams, goals, responsibilities and relationships because they lack patience and the power to persevere. Don't give up on yourself and your goals no matter what life may throw at you. The power of perseverance achieves great results.

RAISE
THE BAR

*Never apologize for setting high
standards for yourself.*

Never apologize for setting high standards for yourself. Setting standards for yourself and those around you sends a distinct message to the world that you value yourself, your time and that of others. You realize that your life has meaning as well as purpose. Your relationships operate only under authenticity, respect and trust. Those who often set high standards for themselves tend to be highly selective in choosing those with whom they share their lives with.

By operating on higher standards, you continue to raise the bar higher. You raise the bar higher for yourself, friends, family and others. Every area in your life is challenged to do its best. In order to achieve your goals and produce effective work, you must challenge yourself. Reading the biographies of past and present global leaders in the fields of business, politics, technology, science and other professional sectors, will reveal to you that they all share a common thread: high standards.

I believe that the whole point of life is to produce greatness—to be excellent at what you do, to master an art, to excel in education, to become a better person, to reach the heights of our most inspirational leaders and make a profound difference in small steps.

Encourage yourself to be better in all aspects. Do not settle for less because less is not good enough. Do not settle for being mediocre when you were born to be extraordinary. The potential to be great and to do greater things rests in your hands. Give yourself the opportunity to put your best self forward.

Each of us has talents, skills and gifts that have not been tapped into yet. Find out what those talents are and use them to make a difference. Be inspired by those who decided to live their lives abundantly. Find inspiration in your experiences and journey through life. Use past disappointments, failures and betrayals to motivate you to achieve greater things. Do not let those emotions slow you down or hinder your growth. No one can go back and make a brand new start, anyone can start from now and make a brand new ending. Every situation or circumstance is an opportunity to do better and be better.

By challenging yourself, you are essentially aligning your thoughts to produce action. Your personal and public mantra should be, "Raise the Bar." Canadian entrepreneur Brian Tracy states, "You can become an even more excellent person by constantly setting higher and higher standards for yourself and then by doing everything possible to live up to those standards."

This is a time for change, a change to make a difference, a time to ignore the naysayers and press forward. Even when the road might seem uncertain, go forward anyway. When you believe that God has your destiny in his hands, nothing can deter you. When you put your faith and dependence solely on God or whoever you are spiritually connect to, how can you not accomplish your goals?

It is important that we remind ourselves of the goals at hand. Keep your eye on the prize and do not be scared to shine and live out your destiny. You are meant to shine brightly and stand out. As Author Marianne Williamson said, "Your playing small does not serve the world." It is because of your existence that the world will become a better place.

As young women we must rise up to the occasion of being Great. We must acquire the attitude, the likeness and the mindset of being excellent. This is not a pursuit of perfection, but a pursuit of greatness. Those who are great are never perfect, and those who are perfect are non-existent. We need to internalize this idea of being excellent. Not many folks spend time trying to be excellent. There is no room for just being mediocre, sitting on the sideline or letting life pass you by. The world is interested in extraordinary people who out of ordinary circumstances, decided to be the change they wanted to see in the world. I believe that there is a special mission that must be done only through you. Remember that each of us has a special mission that has to be done here on Earth.

DON'T BE AFRAID TO SHINE AND STAND OUT

Never downplay what you have been blessed with.

A uthor Marianne Williamson said it best. "Our deepest fear is not that we are inadequate. Our deepest fear is that we are powerful beyond measure. It is our light, not our darkness that most frightens us. We ask ourselves, 'Who am I to be brilliant, gorgeous, talented, fabulous?' Actually, who are you not to be? You are a child of God. Your playing small does not serve the world. There is nothing enlightened about shrinking so that other people won't feel insecure around you. We are all meant to shine, as children do. We were born to make manifest the glory of God that is within us. It's not just in some of us; it's in everyone. And as we let our own light shine, we unconsciously give other people permission to do the same. As we are liberated from our own fear, our presence automatically liberates others."

At times it is hard for young women today to be themselves boldly. If one is physically attractive, intelligent or talented sometimes they feel they must hide or tone down their attributes to make other people feel comfortable around them. There is nothing you can do to make people comfortable around you when they are not comfortable with themselves. You are beautiful, intelligent, wise, talented and so much more than you give yourself credit for, you are doing the world a disservice by hiding or belittling your gifts.

Never downplay what you have been blessed with. Your gifts, talents and purpose are qualities needed to change the world. People all over the world are depending on your gifts. You may possess the next big invention, the next medical cure or be the next political or social leader. Your gifts and talents will serve a far greater purpose but these things can only be achieved if you let your gifts blossom! Insecurity breeds from lack of confidence or assurance of self. Insecurity has no age; sometimes you may meet people far older than you who seem to become intimidated or insecure when they are around you. You may be a simple person, but those who are insecure will always find and see something better in others rather than in themselves. Honestly, it is not the external features that cause people to feel such a way; it is the greatness or potential that is within you. Even the most confident people may feel inferior around someone who boldly lets their light and talent shine, because no one can compete with one's inner light. When your light shines brightly, people have no choice but to be drawn unto you. Each and every one of us has this divine beam of light that transcends all darkness. But most of us have not found it yet or have unconsciously turned it off due to our own attitudes about ourselves. You cannot control the way people feel;

however, never give anyone the power to diminish your gifts. Be bold and never be scared to speak up, stand out and shine. As you let your own light shine you empower others to do the same. You empower them to find their own confidence to shine as well. I want you to promise yourself and me one thing: that you will harness the divine power and light that is within you.

10

THE LAW OF ATTRACTION

Whatever you think, however you see yourself and wherever you envision yourself going, is what will manifest in real terms.

Have you heard about the law of attraction? The Law Attraction goes a little something like this: whatever you think, however you see yourself and wherever you envision yourself going, is what will manifest in real terms. The law of attraction simply states that if you think negatively, you will attract negative outcomes but if you think positively then you will attract all that is positive.

The Law of Attraction is real, more real than I ever imagined. Best selling author Louise Hay, considered mother of positive thinking says: "Every time we think a thought, every time we speak a word, the universe is listening and responding to us." If you constantly find yourself disappointed or pessimistic then you should examine your thought process. Do you constantly doubt yourself? Or think about the "what ifs" before you even start? Then these thoughts could be hindering your progress. What you think will manifest into who you are and how the world will perceive you.

It's time for you to transition your mind. It's time for you to make that transition into positive thinking. You need to realize that you are the heir of all things lofty, noble and great. You must change your mindset from limited thinking to kingdom thinking. Don't worry about your current circumstance or situation. Don't determine your future destination by your current location. You are in the midst of transitioning into something greater.

I strongly believe that when you have positive thoughts you begin to realize that you have everything you need to realize and seize the opportunities in front of you and make your own unique mark. Life is what you make it; don't limit your life by limited thinking. Think BIG, Dream BIG, and Live BIG. By thinking bigger and greater things for yourself, you will begin to attract bigger and better things. Transitioning into your greatness has a lot to do with your mindset and attitude. Limited thinking stunts growth and demobilizes your ability to move forward.

You must put into action every good thought and every inspiring dream. Do not settle for less. Do not sell yourself short. You are meant to manifest and live out the glory that God has intended for you. You have every right to be great, bold, beautiful, excellent, wealthy, intelligent, and more. **Think BIG, Dream BIG, and Live BIG.**

What we tell ourselves on a daily basis has a direct impact on our attitude and thought process. What we feel about ourselves also has an impact on how we carry ourselves and ultimately treat others. Let's start off with something small, read a positive quote or affirmation everyday for the next two months. It will put your mind in line with positive thinking. Say to yourself every day words of affirmation so that you begin to internalize it.

A GOOD NAME
IS PRICELESS

*People will know who you are first
by what they hear from others and
secondly by what they see you do.*

Proverbs 22:1 says, "If you have to choose between a good reputation and great wealth, choose a good reputation."
Wealth may vanish over night, but a good name lasts forever. Living in our society today, there are so many temptations that may lead one into making regrettable decisions.

I cannot stress how important it is to maintain a good name. Although people make mistakes, there are some mistakes that are hard to mend or recover from. Life is like walking on a tightrope making sure we take the right steps so that we don't fall! Which is the same as maintaining good character. People will know who you are first by what they hear from others, and secondly by what they see you do.
The two most important elements of a person are their character and reputation. Your character is made up of distinctive traits, qualities and or abilities that describe/represent who you are.

Your reputation is the estimation in which you are being held. In essence, your reputation stems from your perceived character. Which means you cannot have a reputation without character and you cannot have character that does not produce some sort of a reputation. Your character is your daily display of who you are to the world even when no one is looking.

We sometimes seem to forget the importance of good character and reputation. Why is good character important? Character is like a church bell that rings very loud and grabs everyone's attention. It is like a sign plastered on your forehead for everyone to read. Everything you do and say is a reflection of your character. The problem with society is that we are so eager to look for talent regardless of character. We want the best singers, doctors, politicians, actors, community organizers, professors, scholars and so much more, irrespective of their character at times. Entrepreneur John Luther states, "Good character is more to be praised than outstanding talent. Most talents are, to some extent, a gift. Good character, by contrast, is not given to us. We have to build it piece by piece—by thought, choice, courage and determination."

Our society needs people who are intelligent and talented in the best professions and positions life has to offer and who are also thoughtful, compassionate, empathic, moral, ethical and possess integrity and honesty. As a young woman I ask you to put as much time into the building of your character as you do in the development of your professional goals.

Remember talent is what will get you there but character will keep you there.

12

DON'T TAKE NO FOR AN ANSWER

We need to see every NO as a YES and every opportunity in life whether good or bad as a means to achieving and experiencing happiness.

No, is a word that you will hear often throughout your journey of womanhood, but do not be discouraged. Often we dwell so much on the word NO, that it hinders our mind, body and soul from receiving. Success has no limits when you are able to focus on the positive! We focus on all the NOs in the world and become discouraged and frightened to say just say YES. Everything that we come across in the world pushes us further away from saying yes and pushes us closer to saying no. We are often perplexed, discouraged, and frightened to step out into the unknown and to experience great things that life has to offer.

In order to experience the good of life, we need to change our thinking. We need to see every NO as a YES and every opportunity in life whether good or bad as a means to achieving and experiencing happiness. When you resolve in yourself that no matter what your current situation or surrounding circumstances tell you, you must always see the YES side of it. For every NO there is a YES!

Success has no limits, and success is not scared of NO. Success laughs at difficulty, idleness, discouragement, and roadblocks. A successful person is one who has the ability to turn every No into a Yes. She has the ability to turn the bad into good, to make a meal into a feast and to turn an ordinary life into an extraordinary journey. Be a YES person today, and I guarantee you that your life will change for the better.

There is power in knowing what you want and letting the world know exactly what it is you desire and need. We all have lofty dreams and desires and simple wants and needs, which at times cannot be produced by our own efforts alone. You need to realize that your desires, wants and needs are at times in the hands of someone else. It may be a complete stranger, friend, co-worker, boss, colleague or family-member who knows the answer, holds the key, or has the map to show you the way. But, how will anyone know what it is you need, want or desire if you don't ask or speak up.

At times we can become so arrogant in our talents, skills, knowledge and experience that we forget to ask for help. We believe that we can do it all on our own. Sometimes you need to ask your boss for a raise or a promotion even if you feel they should already know. Sometimes you need to bring attention to whatever it is you feel is already evident. Sometimes you need to just simply ask or tell. Do not be afraid to say what it is you feel and want. If you believe then you will receive. The universe does not have a choice but to align with your wishes and commands.

Author Lois P. Frankel said it best: "Nice girls don't ask, but smart women do. Nice girls don't get the corner office." Its great to be nice, but you need to be nice and smart; you need to be strategic. In essence, be bold, be powerful and speak up. You have every right to experience the fruits of your labor. Don't underestimate the power of asking or the power of people to give you exactly what it is you want and DESERVE! BE BOLD and JUST ASK!

13

FIRST IMPRESSIONS

Your appearance and demeanor speaks volumes.

F irst impressions are everything. This is not shallow; this is reality! First impressions cannot be written off. That is why you must carry yourself at all times with grace, style and confidence. We live in a society where we do judge a book by its cover and I would be lying to you if I said the opposite. In our society, split decisions to hire or associate with someone are based on a few initial factors. When you meet people for the first time, they do not know how many degrees you have, how many languages you speak or what different countries you've traveled to; all they see is you and your appearance. And people make judgments on how you carry yourself, what you wear and your mannerisms.

When you walk into an office for an internship or job interview, let's assume the employer has not seen your curriculum vitae or resume yet. Before you even introduce yourself, the employer has already assessed you from head to toe. He or she has assessed your wardrobe to see if it is professional and appropriate; they look to see if your hair is appropriately kept and how much make-up you wear. Believe it or not, this assessment to others tells a lot about you.

Take control of how the world views you. Your style and fashion choices express your individuality as well as who you are. It can paint you into many things. It tells the world how unique, creative, mundane or sloppy you are. It is true that no matter how you dress, it will always be open to misinterpretation or criticism; however, you still need to be strategic and versatile in your fashion choices.

At the end of the day, your clothes don't carry you; you carry the clothes. So only you can give sunshine to your style. Only you can dictate to fashion what your message is. And your style is a response to who you are, where you want to go and your current place in the world.

If you show up very detail oriented, you're ironed to perfection, your hair looks great straight, curly or natural, your make-up is natural looking yet still feminine and your nails are appropriate and clean—all this will say a lot. It says that as an employee you are very detailed oriented, execute tasks to perfection and probably possess good organizational skills. If on the other hand you come very sloppy, not enough detail and time has been given to your over all look or appearance, the employer may assume things about you that may not be true. These are ways in which you are unknowingly being secretly assessed. You may think your resume may be the persuading factor. But, remember you are the ultimate persuading factor.

Take this advice and use it as a tool/strategy in your journey to success. Take care of yourself and learn the ins and outs of corporate, academic and social life. Watch your manners—say thank you and you're welcome at all times. First impressions matter a lot, so always give and look your best. After all, the best is already in you. Spend time also grooming yourself internally. However you feel about yourself on the inside is what will show on the outside. Always take care of your outer and inner beauty. Always.

14

SHOW ME YOUR FRIENDS...

Show me your friends and I will show you who you are.

S how me your friends and I will show you who you are," is a saying that I think we all are familiar with. Who you choose to surround yourself with is a direct reflection of who you are. It really is. In order to understand the concept of, "Show me your friends and I will show you who you are," you must first understand the definition of a friend. A friend is someone with whom you share a mutual affection, association or bond. People choose their friends for various reasons such as shared interests, commonalities, need, professional pursuits and more. However, one thing to be remembered is that people enter into friendships because he or she represents something within you.

You may be judged by the company that you keep because there is also a saying that goes, "guilty by association." The people you associate with especially for over a long period of time are able to influence you in ways in which you may not even realize. They are able to use their position or duration in your life to sway your opinions, affect your decision making and most significantly, change the course of your future for better or worse.

Many of us have been blessed to have good friends. But, many of us have had our share of bad friendships. We've spent months, years and maybe seasons sharing our lives with people who should not have had a seat in our lives. I learned back in high school that I would rather be alone than surrounded by other women who were not truly happy for me, secretly envied me or always felt the need to compete. At an early age, I hated cliques and became very comfortable with myself and being by myself.

One thing I know for sure is that people come into your life for many reasons. Some to help you, others to learn from you, some to hold you back and others to push you forward. You have to recognize that not all friends serve the same purpose. Some are just there to go to social events with; I call them social friends. Some are there to study with; I call those study buddies. Others are there to pray with and really talk about serious issues; I call those counselor friends. Some are there to gossip and turn small issues into gigantic ones; I call those drama queens. You will come across all types of friends but do not expect everyone to meet your point of needs or expectations.

Always ask yourself, "What type of company do I keep?" Have I grown maturely and positively with this friend? Does this friendship force me to be a better person? It is essential to always evaluate the company you keep. People have the power to empower and dis-empower. People can build you up to tear you down. Choose wisely and pick selectively when it comes to the company you keep. Do I surround myself with people as passionate as I am or am I surrounded by people who are mediocre and satisfied with where they are now? Do ambitious people or those who lack drive and persistence surround me? Do I eat and dine with those who have questionable motives? These are questions you need to ask yourself. It's not about being paranoid or judgmental, it's about making the best decisions for you. The road to success and the journey of womanhood requires vision, wisdom and action. You must envision yourself at the finish line before you get there. You must have wisdom to make the right decisions even down to picking friends. You must take action: uproot those who will not take you closer to your goals. Help those who are seeking to experience the best out of their lives. And take full responsibility for the relationships you nurture and let go.

One important thing I also learned is to be good friends with oneself. Be the type of friend you dreamed of always having, the type of friend that has all the qualities to make it with you to the mountaintops. As a woman, you should not expect others to treat you in ways that you cannot treat yourself or those around you.

The importance of keeping good company is essential. The road to success is not an individual journey. Success is not an isolated experience; it is the cumulative effort of hundreds maybe thousands of people who will usher you into your destiny. You must surround yourself with people as motivated and passionate as you are. You will never find sheep playing with wolves nor can you find night and day during the same time. You owe more to yourself and your future. Do not let the company you keep delay or hinder you from experiencing your best self. Surround yourself with positive and genuine people. Be around people who are first self-motivated then people-motivated. Those people will serve as your support cast, and genuinely be happy with the decisions you make for your own life and the goals that you continue to accomplish. People who are self-motivated do not really need other people to reinforce their greatness; they already know it themselves. They tend to learn from people and adopt skills and techniques from others that will help in assisting them to better themselves and others. Surround yourself with them.

In the end, one must be their own best friend and know what it is they want and expect out of the relationships they cultivate. Learn to appreciate those who open their lives and hearts to you.

Remember, while being a good friend to yourself, do not push people away. Remain open and willing to create, mend and build new relationships.

15

DECISIONS DETERMINE YOUR OUTCOME

Decision making is what shapes the lives we ultimately wish to live.

K nowing when to make the right decisions is a tough task. Which way should you go? Do you go right or left? Life is all about making decisions, but how do you know when you're making the right decision? One must factor all foreseeable obstacles, outcomes, advantages and disadvantages when making a decision. One must also understand that external advice can only do so much. Ultimately, your gut instincts, intuition and concrete factors will help you in effective decision making.

Every day we make decisions. Decisions on what to eat, what to wear, what to say, what to do, what to buy, what not to say, how not to act, where to go, what to accomplish, who to date, who to marry, where to work, where to move. Our lives are full of decision-making. In the midst of this daily routine, its important to understand that decision-making is what shapes the lives we ultimately wish to live. Napoleon Bonaparte said it best: "Nothing is more difficult, and therefore more precious, than to be able to decide."

For each decision you make in life whether big or small there is also a consequence. At times, we tend to think of consequences as having a bad connotation but in retrospect a consequence is an outcome or result of an action and this can either be good or bad. As you grow older you will realize how much making the right decision the first time around can change the course of things greatly.

When I say making the "right" decision, I mean making decisions that are reflective of who you are, and most importantly, making decisions that you are at peace with. We seldom make "right" decisions, but we must learn how to make our own decisions so that we can be at peace with them. How many times do you factor in everyone else opinions on what you should do instead of looking into yourself for the answer? Making the right decision does not necessarily mean that it will work out the way you planned but at least you were able to make a decision that is reflective of who you are.

Here are 5 steps that I believe will bring you closer to effective decision-making and fulfilling your goals.

1. **Know Your End Goal.**
What is it that you want to accomplish? Determine if your decision will bring you closer to your goal.

2. Weigh Your Options.

Sit back and think about the advantages and disadvantages of making such a decision. If the good outweighs the bad then go for it and if not then take more time to think about it.

3. Be Strategic.

Make decisions that are strategic. Does your decision put you directly in line with your goal? Analyze foreseeable outcomes and factors.

4. Listen to Yourself.

Advice is great but following your own instincts is even greater. Be open to advice and use that information in helping you make better decisions. Remember, it's not about always making the "right" the decision; it's also about making decisions that you will be at peace with.

5. Accept the Outcome.

You may have an idea of how things may pan out when making a certain decision, but when it does not result into the outcome you were looking for, take responsibility for it. You can either accept the outcome or work towards changing it.

16

KNOW
YOUR WORTH

Knowing your worth means that you value your time, your experiences, your knowledge, you're uniqueness and your body.

K nowing your worth means understanding that you have and **bring** value to the world. At times, as young women, you may find yourself in situations that question who you are, challenge you to compromise your values or make decisions that do not honor who you are. You have to know that you matter.

I learned that knowing my worth goes far beyond just thinking it or saying it; I must act on it. Knowing your worth means that you value your time, your experiences, your knowledge, you're uniqueness and your body. The value that you have for your self will also apply to your relationships. Honoring yourself means that you are making a conscious effort to seek and build relationships with people who respect you and value your friendship or courtship.

Never lower your standards to impress anyone. You are unique, special and one of a kind and that is more than enough. Not everyone will like you for just being you, but that should not stop you from expressing and embracing your individuality. Knowing your worth means that regardless of criticism, you are able to turn critique into constructive counsel and are able to still maintain who you are.

Do not let anyone make you feel less than who you are. The journey of womanhood is filled with making mistakes and growing pains. Embrace your failures and mistakes, for they will build you into a stronger person. Your experiences both personally and professionally are also worthy and have value; never compare your achievements to those of offers. By doing so, you discount your own unique journey and the experiences you have along the way which have contributed to your growth.

As you continue to rise in the ranks of your professional career, hold your values close to your heart. Write a list of things that you will not compromise under any circumstances. Most importantly, put self-love and self-worth at the top of your list. Knowing your worth means that you love and respect your self first and foremost. In order to teach people how to treat you, you must show the example by first treating yourself with love and respect.

17

HUMILITY

*You see, humility is concerned about
the outcome of the act, while ego or arrogance
are more concerned about the act or the person
committing it.*

Humility does not mean thinking less of yourself it means you think of yourself less. Why is humility important? Sometimes one may get so caught up in their own goals, ambitions, talents and achievements, they forget that it's not all about them. Humility allows you to think outside of yourself and see yourself as a form of service.

I believe that your talents and gifts will always make room for you. I also believe that your talents and gifts are a form of service to the world, which serves a far greater purpose. It's okay to bask in your accomplishments but it's not okay to think that you are better than anyone else. Humility is concerned about the outcome of the act, while ego or arrogance is more concerned about the act or the person committing it.

Don't get caught up in your own abilities; be more concerned about how your ability can make a difference, solve a problem or provide a solution to something other than yourself. It's a great feeling when you are operating in purpose, because your purpose will always come in the form of service that will impact something or someone's life.

It is important to find a balance between thinking you're great without being overly proud and self-centered. Always believe that you are put on this earth for a far greater purpose than just yourself. Think of humility as a pathway to selflessness and increase of service and social responsibility.

18

DON'T TAKE CRITICISM PERSONALLY

I had a hard time for a while understanding that not all criticism was a personal attack on me.

I had a hard time for a while understanding that not all criticism was a personal attack on me. I would often sit and listen to a mentor, family friend, associate, professional colleague say things to me that I perceived to be rude or disrespectful yet really was just constructive advice not presented on a silver platter.

Not all criticism should be taken so personally. At times criticism from the other person may come from a gritty not so genuine place and at times it may come from a sincere place, but the delivery may be all wrong. I learned and I am still learning that criticism will not always be in the form we want or expect. Also, never let criticism or critique crush your spirit. You have to be able to take it in stride and keep moving forward.

You will meet people you admire and those who feel the need to check you, critique your path, question your decision-making, belittle your ambitions or insult your way of doing things; whatever it may be, do not take it personally. Learn to keep a protective shield around your spirit while also maintaining the ability to listen attentively to what is being said. Sometimes the key to understanding whether one's criticism is actually genuine or sincere is through listening to your gut and paying attention to your instincts. Your inner voice will tell whether such advice is coming from a good place or a broken one.

Remember, that people will give advice by using their own personal experiences, perceptions and values. At times, all three areas will not align with yours or be suitable for you. Learn how to pick and choose which advice or critique should apply to you. It's not an easy thing to do; it is truly a process.

I suffered through some serious heartaches thinking about some of the criticism and professional and even personal critiques that I received in certain situations. Now, I've learned not to take it personally, to be resilient, to roll with the punches and keep moving forward. After all, that's life. Look at the positive side of criticism; there is something to be learned.

19

HAVE
A VISION

*I had a vision for my life.
I did not quite know how I would
achieve those things, but what I
know now is that my vision has
guided me to where I am now.*

I n order to know exactly what is you want out of life, you must first have a vision of what you want your life to be. You will hear people ask you, "What do you want to be?" Or, "What is it that you want out of life?" These questions, however, are not easy to answer until you have some sort of vision first.

I consider myself to be many things: an educator, a scholar, a writer, a philanthropist, a humanitarian, a leadership expert, and as I get older the list gets longer. As a young girl, I had a vision for my life. I saw myself as a President or Ambassador of a country. I saw myself in high-level positions where I was integral in changing lives. I even analyzed the lives of Oprah Winfrey, Nelson Mandela, and other political and social leaders because I wanted to examine their road to success. I had a vision for my life. I did not quite know how I would achieve those things, but what I know now is that my vision has guided me to where I am now.

I can say with confidence that I am all those things that I mentioned, because I strongly believe that we are more than just one title or one profession; but we are a myriad of things—a myriad of talents, gifts, professions and more that make up who we are in this world, and it's okay to embrace all of the unique things about you.

Having a vision for your life is essential. It's that guiding light that reminds you to stay on course. It teaches you be resilient and helps you define who you are. Vision is something no one can take from you. Only you own the vision of your life. And it's up to you to put in the work to have that vision come to fruition.

20

ALWAYS
BE GRATEFUL

Be thankful for everything and every person who comes into your life

B e grateful for every stage of life that you experience. Gratitude unlocks the door of gratefulness. There is power in being grateful. Being grateful means that you appreciate and have a sense of gratitude for everything that comes your way. Being grateful opens the door to more opportunities and blessings, and it shuts the door of hopelessness and discontent. Many of us go through life complaining and not realizing how blessed and lucky we are. If you stop and think for a second about how lucky, blessed and favored you are despite it all, you will begin to realize that instead of focusing on the negative in life.

When you adopt a sense of gratefulness, you begin to realize that all good and bad things have actually worked in your favor. It has further developed your character and increased your perseverance. When you are grateful, you are able to see the positive in every negative situation. You realize that there is a lesson to be learned in all experiences in life and are grateful for the many lessons learned.

By being grateful you are able to understand that your level of success is not by your own doing alone. I believe that no man is an island; we are all tiny fabrics woven together resulting in a beautiful quilt. Our lives are like that of quilts, and people, things, experiences, open doors, shut doors, criticism, advice, opportunities all add to the make-up of unique quilts.

Be thankful for everything and every person who comes into your life. And always show your appreciation. Proper etiquette is acknowledging others, showing appreciation and saying thank you. These three things may not seem like a big deal but they are. When you consciously make an effort to show appreciation, you are training your mind, body and spirit to be grateful and to always express your gratitude.

Remember, gratefulness turns what we have into enough.

About the Author

Yetunde A. Odugbesan-Omede is a Professor of Global Affairs and Political Science. She is the Founder of Young Woman's Guide, Inc., an organization that provides young women around the world with leadership development. She is the CEO of Yetunde Global Consulting, a management consulting firm that specializes in leadership development and training, organizational management and global business strategies. She earned her undergraduate degree in Journalism and Media Studies and her graduate degrees in Global Affairs at Rutgers University. She holds numerous awards and certificates in Leadership and Applied Politics. Yetunde speaks and conducts seminars worldwide on human rights, leadership and women/ youth empowerment. She resides in New York with her husband and son.

Learn more about Yetunde at:
www.yetundeodugbesan.com

CPSIA information can be obtained
at www.ICGtesting.com
Printed in the USA
LVHW070620090420
652774LV00001B/15

* 9 7 8 0 6 9 2 3 2 2 9 5 6 *